NULLIFYING
FEDERAL AND STATE
GUN CONTROL

NULLIFYING
FEDERAL AND STATE
GUN CONTROL
A HOW-TO GUIDE FOR GUN OWNERS

JAMES RONALD KENNEDY

SHOTWELL
COLUMBIA · So. CAR.
EST. 2015
PUBLISHING

For rights and permissions, please contact:

SHOTWELL PUBLISHING, LLC
PO Box 2592
Columbia, SC 29202

www.shotwellpublishing.com | info@shotwellpublishing.com

ISBN: 978-1-947660-60-1

10 9 8 7 6 5 4 3 2 1

TABLE OF CONTENTS

Chapter 1

FREEDOM REQUIRES GUNS
IN THE HANDS OF LAW-ABIDING CITIZENS

> If ye love wealth better than liberty, the tranquility of servitude, than the animating contest of freedom —go from us in peace. We ask not your counsels or arms. Crouch down and lick the hands which feed you. May your chains set lightly upon you, and may posterity forget that ye were our countrymen.

—Samuel Adams, August 1, 1776.

GUN OWNERSHIP IN AMERICA is far higher than any other nation in the world—around 90 guns per 100 population. According to liberals, progressives, and other assorted leftist—best described as neo-Marxists—this is the reason for America's high murder rate. How does "gun crazy" America's murder rate stack-up against other nations, especially those that have very restrictive gun control laws? A study of the murder rate per 100,000 population prepared in 2015 demonstrated that the U.S.A. was NOT the number one murder capital of the world. The number one murder capital of the world was Honduras and number two was Venezuela. Both of these nations have very restrictive gun control laws. Gun-loving U.S.A. came in as number 111 out of 218 countries. And this is not the end of the story! If you remove gun violence that occurs daily in Democratic-controlled cities from the U.S. data, then the murder rate plumets to almost the bottom of the list![1] So the incessant demand for gun control by neo-Marxists in the political arena, the media, and academia is fueled by crimes committed in cities controlled by Democrats! They, the neo-Marxists, have created the very problem that they are now using as an excuse to disarm law-abiding Americans! Guns are not the source of the problem— it's the people. The U.S.A. does not have a gun violence problem, we have a people problem. The problem lies with the people who vote without thinking about the long-term impact their vote will have on their community, the people in elected offices who pass ideologically-driven laws and leftist social policies, and the people who run these death-producing cities. These death-producing cities could not exist without the support of neo-Marxist politicians in Washington, DC.

MORE GUN CONTROL RESULTS IN MORE CRIME

According to the federal government there were 19,141 deaths in America attributed to "assault or homicide" in 2019.[2] Early FBI statistics indicate a 25% increase in the murder rate in 2020—which is higher than the rate for 2019.[3] And this increase arose during the government-enforced COVID lockdowns! The trend for more gun control and rising crime has been ongoing for decades. From 1973 to 1991, 36.6 million Americans were injured as a result of violent crime. One in four households in America was victimized by criminals. Yet the left-of-center, neo-Marxist politicians at the federal and, increasingly at the state level, are constantly demanding that law-abiding Americans surrender their right to keep and bear arms. The neo-Marxist attack against the Second Amendment is reaching near fever pitch. When the day comes that the neo-Marxists feel confident that they now have

---

1 Bill Whittle on Firewall, https://www.youtube.com/watch?v=pELwCqz2JfE accessed 10/20/2020.

2 https://www.cdc.gov/nchs/fastats/homicide.htm accessed 8/2/2021.

3 https://www.vox.com/22344713/murder-violent-crime-spike-surge-2020-covid-19-coronavirus accessed 8/2/2021.

secure control of the Senate, they will move to pack the Supreme Court with "liberal" or "progressive" justices. These new justices will be expected to uphold federal legislation that will essentially nullify the Second Amendment. If we don't act decisively, soon the Second Amendment will have no more power to protect us from an oppressive federal government than the Ninth and Tenth Amendments have in protecting States' Rights!

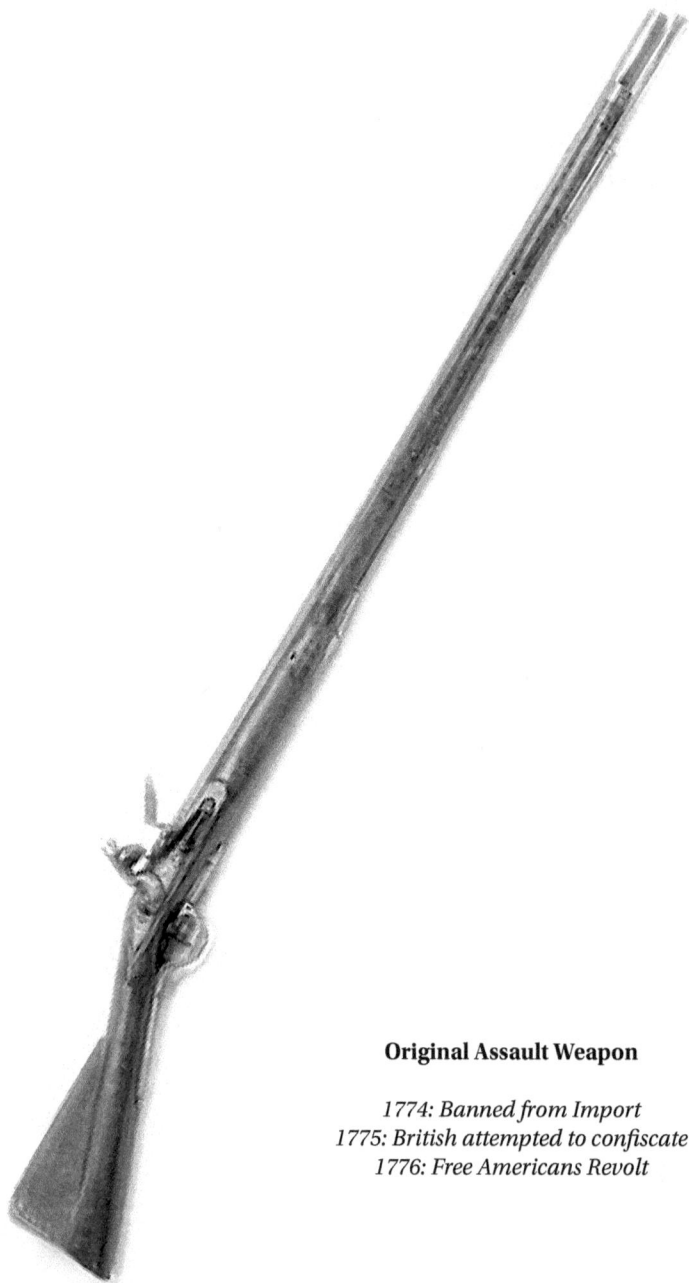

Original Assault Weapon

1774: Banned from Import
1775: British attempted to confiscate
1776: Free Americans Revolt

Chapter 2

Deep State Politicians Are Making War On The Second Amendment

IN HIS FIRST ADDRESS TO CONGRESS after his questionable election, Joe Biden openly declared war against our rights under the Second Amendment. He specifically noted his intentions to limit gun magazine capacity to no more than 10 rounds. [1] As we all know the typical magazine capacity of popular handguns is well above 10 rounds. With a House and Senate controlled by left-of-center Democrats who follow the demands of America's vocal neo-Marxists, and a President who is nothing more than a mouthpiece for his neo-Marxist puppet masters, our Second Amendment rights are in grave danger **if** we do nothing different from what we have been doing to defeat the neo-Marxist gun grabbers. Neo-Marxist politicians and social justice warriors are also attacking gun rights by attempting to limit availability of ammunition via taxes, regulations, and threats of suits against both gun and ammunition manufacturers. Unfortunately, we cannot rely solely on our "friends" in the Republican Party to defend us against these neo-Marxist gun grabbers.

---

1   https://www.nraila.org/articles/20210503/biden-goes-all-in-on-calls-for-extreme-gun-control accessed 5/5/2021.

DEMOCRATS AND REPUBLICANS MOVING AGAINST THE SECOND AMENDMENT

In the month of July 2021, the city of Chicago had 461 shootings. Chicago is a Democrat-controlled city with some of the strictest gun-control city ordinances anywhere in the U.S. Yet, Democrat Mayor Lori Lightfoot is calling for more gun control legislation at the federal level.[2] This is typical of the neo-Marxists' use of violence they allow to occur within cities they control and then use this violence as an excuse to push efforts to disarm law-abiding Americans.

The Chicago *Sun-Times*, in a report updated August 2, 2021, reported that in the last six years of shootings, over 1000 people were injured and hundreds killed. During this time the liberal (neo-Marxist) officials of Chicago have only managed to produce two convictions![3] Chicago ended 2020 with a grand total of 769 homicides.[4] And yet their answer to violent crime in gun-control Chicago is to attack your Second Amendment rights! Neo-Marxists are not concerned about controlling criminals but they are very determined to control law-abiding, conservative Americans.

The problem is not just a problem with leftist ideologues who control the Democrat Party—Republicans are just as guilty. They either endorse "compromise" gun-control legislation or, at times, they actually become the deciding votes in passing such legislation. Recently eight Republicans helped Democrats pass Biden-supported gun-control legislation in the House of Representatives.[5] As one "conservative" from Oklahoma admitted when asked how he manages to get along in a liberal-controlled Congress and still get reelected,

---

2 https://www.breitbart.com/politics/2021/06/16/mayor-lori-lightfoot-seeks-federal-gun-control-as-chicago-shootings-surge/ accessed 8/2/2021.

3 https://chicago.suntimes.com/crime/2021/8/2/22559312/mass-shooting-victims-gun-violence-crime-cpd-police-department-clearance-murder-arrest accessed 8/3/2021.

4 https://apnews.com/article/homicide-chicago-violence-coronavirus-pandemic-gun-violence-be4b972267e31358dd165925d5a33cce accessed 8/6/2021.

5 https://www.breitbart.com/politics/2021/03/11/8-house-republicans-vote-for-democrat-gun-control-bill/ accessed 8/2/2021.

"You have to talk conservative when you are back home and vote with the liberals when you are in Washington." This is the routine manner in which "our" politicians rule over us. Notice how that even though a majority of Americans are opposed to illegal immigration, Congress never acts to stop it. Why? Because the Democrats need the illegals who will vote for the Democrats and the Republicans are indebted to special interest groups—their big money donors of the Chamber of Commerce, Wall Street, and Globalists who want cheap labor. These special-interest groups have a government to promote their interests while "We the people" are stateless—we have no government to protect and promote our interests.

LEFTIST POLITICAL ELITES PROTECT NEO-MARXIST DOMESTIC TERRORISTS

The neo-Marxist media and politicians have had a field-day using the events of January 6, 2021 as evidence of their claim that there exists today in America a danger of a right-wing, domestic-terrorist plot to overthrow the nation's civil government.[6] Yet, the neo-Marxists had very few complaints when leftwing groups actually bombed the U.S. Capitol—not once but twice! Neo-Marxists always have selective outrage. They are outraged if a drug-crazed black man is shot and killed by police while trying to apprehend the criminal but they are silent when black criminals or mobs attack and kill whites. Leftwing outrage is reserved for those cases that they can use, via their monopolistic control of the media, to advance their neo-Marxist agenda.

---

6   Many journalists have question whether the FBI acted as agent provocateurs in the events of January 6, 2021. It would not be the first time, see: https://www.revolver.news/2021/06/five-cases-of-fbi-incitement/ accessed 6/22/2021; and https://www.breitbart.com/clips/2021/06/19/fncs-carlson-fbis-focus-on-joe-bidens-political-opponents-a-nightmare-for-civil-liberties-threat-to-democracy/ accessed 6/19/2021.

In 1971 leftwing radicals calling themselves the Weather Underground planted a bomb in the U.S. Capitol.[7] The explosion caused significant damage and shocked average Americans. Supporters of the Weathermen (the same group or a spin-off radical group) were instrumental in promoting and eventually propelling a young black community organizer from Chicago into the U.S. Presidency. Being associated with radicals on the left is no hinderance for neo-Marxist politicians. Now imagine the outcry and rage from the neo-Marxist media if it were discovered that a leading Republican had a remote connection with a rightwing group that used bombs to promote their agenda! Selective outrage is the hallmark of the left.

In 1983 another group of leftwing radicals exploded a bomb inside the U.S. Capitol causing extensive damage. The bombing was conducted by one of America's first female domestic terrorists, Susan Rosenberg.[8] She was convicted and sentenced to 58 years in federal prison. President Bill Clinton commuted her sentence to time served on January 20, 2001. *She is now a major fundraiser for Black Lives Matter!*[9] Again, this points out the selective outrage on the left and this selective outrage goes as high as the President of the U.S.A. Meanwhile, "We the people" have no government to protect and promote our interests. We are a stateless people. The genocide of the Christian Armenian people by the Muslim Turks and the genocide of Jewish people by the Nazis serves as a stark warning to us! Stateless people become easy targets for genocide.

---

7   https://www.politico.com/news/magazine/2021/02/28/when-the-left-attacked-the-capitol-471270 accessed 8/4/2021.

8   https://www.smithsonianmag.com/history/1980s-far-left-female-led-domestic-terrorism-group-bombed-us-capitol-180973904/ accessed 8/4/2021.

9   https://www.kusi.com/retired-nypd-commissioner-bernard-kerik-warns-public-black-lives-matter-fundraising-is-run-by-a-terrorist/ accessed 8/4/2021.

William Rawle wrote the first textbook used to teach the Constitution at West Point Military Academy. He was a firm believer in the Constitutional right of a free people to keep and bear arms as well as the right of Sovereign States to secede from the Union.

Neo-Marxist Bomb U.S. Capitol 1983
President Clinton Released the culprit.

Chapter 3

NEO-MARXIST VIOLENCE AGAINST CONSERVATIVE AMERICANS

IN THE DEBATE OVER GUN CONTROL, we are often asked "Why do law abiding folks needs guns?" The answer is very simple—we need guns because criminals and neo-Marxists are not law-abiding folks! Criminals use violence as a way to take advantage of those they deem weak and unprepared. Neo-Marxists follow Communist Chinese leader Chairman Mao Tse-Tung's axiom that "Political power grows out of the barrel of a gun."[1] In other words, America's neo-Marxists believe that violence is justified if it is used to promote the Marxist revolution. Modern day neo-Marxists, such as Antifa and Black Lives Matter, know that the neo-Marxist media and political class will give them "cover" as they go about attacking conservative Americans who dare to oppose them. CNN even went as far as to claim that people (neo-Marxist no doubt) have a right to harass Trump supporters and run them out of restaurants.[2] A

---

1   Mao Tse-Tung, *Quotations From Chairman Mao Tse-Tung* (Foreign Language Press, Peking, China: 1964), 121. This is the famous "Little Red Book" that launched the Chinese Cultural Revolution during the 1960s in which historic monuments were destroyed, traditions rejected, and thousands of innocent folks were killed by rampaging young people. Similar to what is currently happening in the streets of America.

2   https://www.breitbart.com/big-journalism/2018/10/10/nolte-cnn-says-mobs-have-constitutional-right-to-chase-republicans-out-of-restaurants/   accessed 10/10/2018.

neo-Marxist professor at the University of Mississippi stated that just harassing conservatives was not enough because, "they don't deserve civility."[3] This is the general attitude of all neo-Marxists. Take for example the sad story about a white business owner, Jake Gardner, who used a legally owned weapon to defend his business during a BLM inspired riot in Omaha, Nebraska, May 30, 2020. In a scuffle with a rioter who already had a lengthy criminal record Mr. Gardner, fearing for his life, shot and killed the black rioter. It was later found that the rioter was high on Methamphetamines. The local, neo-Marxist, District Attorney charged Gardner with manslaughter and making terroristic threats! Mr. Gardner lost his business, was harassed and threatened by local neo-Marxists, lost his home, had no money to pay for his legal defense, became depressed and committed suicide. Gardner was an Iraq War veteran.[4] Even though Mr. Gardner had served "his" country during the Iraq War, in reality he was a stateless person—he had no government to protect his interest. This is a warning to all gun owners—we are a stateless people. How "We the people" can correct this major political disadvantage and vulnerability (statelessness) is explained in the second half of this booklet.

In July, 2018, Breitbart news published a list of over 600 cases in which conservatives were attacked by leftwing (neo-Marxist) radicals.[5] The article called out the media for labeling Trump supporters Nazis and white supremacists in an effort to dehumanize conservatives. Conservatives and especially Second Amendment rights advocates must understand that when tyrants want to commit genocide against their opponents, they first dehumanize their opponents. They thereby place their opponents outside the bounds of human compassion—dehumanized, stateless people

---

3   https://www.breitbart.com/tech/2018/10/18/ole-miss-professor-james-thomas-put-your-whole-damn-fingers-in-republicans-meals/ accessed 10/18/2018.

4   Kennedy, James Ronald, *Be Ye Separate-Bible Belt Revival or Marxist Revolution* (Xulon Press, Maitland, FL: 2021), 73.

5   https://www.breitbart.com/the-media/2018/07/05/rap-sheet-acts-of-media-approved-violence-and-harassment-against-trump-supporters/ accessed 7/7/2018.

quickly become victims of genocide.[6] When national presidential candidates used derogatory terms such as "deplorables," "smelly Walmart shoppers," "irredeemables," and "bitter clingers" they are engaging in an active effort to dehumanize their conservative opponents. These terms were not chosen "on the fly." These words were carefully and deliberately chosen in order to convey to their neo-Marxist followers the message that the neo-Marxist ruling elite have declared open season on all conservatives. And conservatives may not admit it but fear of attacks from the neo-Marxist mobs is having its effect. Studies have shown that conservatives have begun to self-censor their formerly free speech.[7] They know that if they speak up the neo-Marxist mobs will target them, their jobs, or their families. Without realizing it, "We the people" have allowed our neo-Marxist enemies to curtail our First Amendment right of Freedom of Speech and Freedom of Expression. This is the reason that we must protect our Second Amendment rights—our neo-Marxist enemies are unscrupulous and blood thirsty.

It must be remembered that it is not the neo-Marxist mobs in the street that present a danger to well-armed Americans—as well armed Americans we can defeat the soy-boy, feminazi, rabble. The real danger arises from the neo-Marxist ruling class that is determined to dehumanize us, disarm us, and then it will be our turn to be assigned to their Killing Fields, their Gulags, or their re-education camps. In a June 18, 2021, column written by Whitney Webb titled "Who Is A Terrorist In Biden's America?" the author issues a warning that all gun owners should take to heart:

> Far from being a war against "white supremacy," the Biden administration's new "domestic terror" strategy clearly targets primarily those who oppose US government overreach and those who oppose capitalism and/or globalization.

---

6   Kennedy & Kennedy, *Yankee Empire: Aggressive Abroad and Despotic At Home* (Shotwell Publishing, Columbia, SC: 2018), 284-5.

7   https://www.ocregister.com/2020/08/14/conservatives-self-censor-and-it-gets-worse-with-more-time-spent-in-college/ accessed 8/5/2021.

The author continues by pointing out how easy it will be for the Biden administration or any other administration to sweep up any political opponent by labeling him or her as a domestic terrorist. What would be your crime? You opposed a specific government policy! What this means is that if a conservative opposes a government rule, regulation, law, or policy by writing blogs or other "online" statements challenging the government, the conservative could be:

> ...deemed to be "inciting" resistance ... could be considered domestic terrorists.[8]

The neo-Marxists who now control the supreme Federal government are developing the unconstitutional machinery to seize law-abiding Americans who disagree with their policy positions.[9] This is not the first time this has happened in the United States—it has happened before and it will happen again if we do nothing to prevent it. This is similar to the bell that Lincoln's Secretary of State, Seward, had on his desk. He bragged to an English journalist that "I can touch a bell on my right hand and order the arrest of a citizen of Ohio. I can touch the bell again and order the arrest of a citizen of New York. Can Queen Victoria do as much?" This was not mere bragging. During the North's invasion of the Confederate States of America hundreds if not thousands of Northerners living under Lincoln's government were arrested by the government and military in plain violation of their Constitutionally protected due process rights. And as Republican President George Bush declared, "If Lincoln did it, then it must be OK."

---

8 Whitney Webb https://www.thelastamericanvagabond.com/who-is-a-terrorist-in-bidens-america/ accessed 6/22/2021.

9 Recall how those who opposed Obama's healthcare plan were labeled "racist" due to their political opposition to Obama's policies. In the future similar labeling could be used to accuse people who oppose federal policy on gun-control as mentally unfit to "keep and bear arms."

Chapter 4

HOW WE CAN DEFEAT FEDERAL AND STATE GUN CONTROL EFFORTS

It is a characteristic of any decaying civilization that the great masses of the people are unaware of the tragedy. Humanity in a crisis is generally insensitive to the gravity of the times in which it lives.

—Archbishop Fulton J. Sheen.

THE NEO-MARXISTS are flexing their political muscle in an effort to disarm law-abiding Americans. They have socialist/communist billionaires financing their efforts; they have the mainline and digital media behind their efforts; they have postmodernist professors in universities across America behind their efforts; and they have the Democratic Party behind their efforts to disarm law-abiding Americans. To make matters worse, all we have to protect our rights is a wimpy, emasculated Republican Party filled with RINOs and counterfeit conservatives.[1] If we are to maintain our Second Amendment rights, we must not rely on the professional political class in the Republican Party. We must do something different, something unlike anything we have done

---

1 A counterfeit conservative is any elected official or party leader who is not actively working for a **fundamental** change in the current supreme Federal government. Specifically, someone who has not endorsed our Sovereign State Amendment (see Chapter 12) and who is not actively working to have the amendment submitted to the States for their ratification.

in the past. In the last part of this booklet, I explain how "We the people" can defeat our neo-Marxist enemies by organizing our own Provisional government in each state and use it to conduct irregular *political* warfare. We can defeat them because we will give them a battle they have never faced! Working together with fellow conservatives in Red State and Red County America we will return the right of local self-government to the people—we will remove power from the Deep State in Washington, DC, and return it to where it belongs—to the people. But first we will establish the fact that "We the people" do indeed have a legal and Constitutional right to keep and bear arms based upon the history of this great Constitutional Republic of Sovereign States.

THE AMERICAN RIGHT TO KEEP AND BEAR ARMS SHALL NOT BE INFRINGED

The right of Americans to keep and bear arms was recognized early in our history. James Madison, known as the Father of the Constitution and future President, declared that tyrants were "afraid to trust the people with arms" and praised our country because of "the advantage of being armed, which the Americans possess over the people of almost every other nation."[2] The Second Amendment's protecting our right to keep and bear arms was described as necessary so that "the Constitution be never construed to prevent the people who are peaceable citizens from keeping their own arms."[3] The great Southern patriot, Patrick Henry, declared that "The great objective is that every man be armed."[4] Note: This is the same Patrick Henry who declared, "Give me liberty or give me death!" and "What I have first at heart is American *liberty;* the second is American *union.*"[5] The meaning of the second quote is that

---

2   Madison, James, *The Federalist* No. 46.

3   Don Kates, **Handgun Prohibition and the Original Meaning of the Second Amendment**, *82 Michigan Law Review* (1983), 203-24.

4   Patrick Henry, quoted in Wayne LaPierre, *Guns, Crime, and Freedom* (Washington, DC: Regnery Publishing, Inc.: 1994), 16-7.

5   Patrick Henry as cited in, Kennedy & Kennedy, *Punished With Poverty-the Suffering South,* 2nd edition (Shotwell Publishing, Columbia, SC: 2020), 6.

Tyrants and Mass Murders Agree

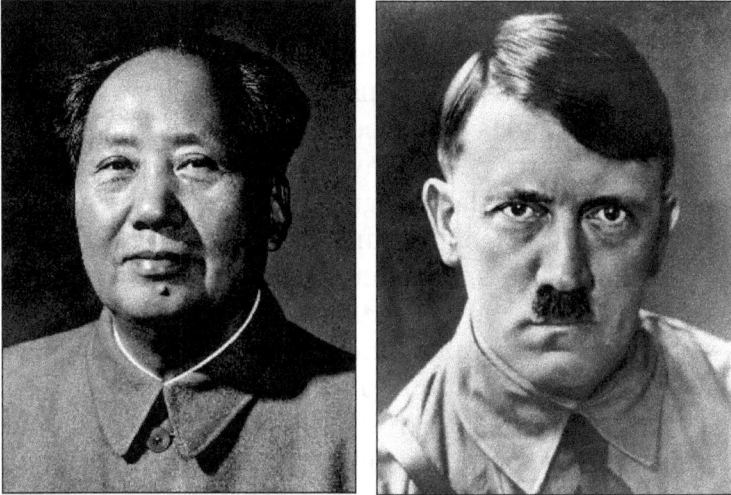

Gun Control Works—For the Tyrants!

liberty always trumps government—any government, especially a government that is attempting to repress Constitutional rights of "We the people."

The writings of the Anti-Federalists of Pennsylvania also demonstrate why maintaining the right to keep and bear arms is important to a free people. "That the people have a right to bear arms to defend themselves and their own state...and no law shall be passed for disarming the people or any of them." The Anti-Federalists were writing during the debate on whether their state should ratify the Constitution. Their main concern was that the proposed Federal government would become too big and begin the process of centralization—the destruction of States' Rights and thereby destroying the ability of the people to protect themselves from an oppressive Federal government. The 1787 warnings of America's Anti-Federalists have become our sad reality.

The right of citizens to keep and bear arms was also recognized after the end of our war with the British Empire. The War for American Independence was a war fought by the British Empire in an effort to prevent the Thirteen Colonies from seceding from the

British Empire. All Empires think their empire is indivisible.[6] The writings of the early Americans who were debating the adoption of the Constitution demonstrate why maintaining the right to bear arms is important for a free people. "That the people have a right to bear arms for the defense of themselves and their own state, or the United States ...and no law shall be passed for disarming the people or any of them..."[7] Free people have the right of self-protection. An early constitutional scholar recognized the importance of firearms in the hands of free men. The first textbook on the Constitution used at West Point Military Academy was written by William Rawle in 1825. He was very clear and to the point regarding the protection afforded by the Second Amendment: "The prohibition is general. No clause in the constitution could by any rule of construction be conceived to give the congress a power to disarm the people." Rawle warns us that "...the prevention of popular insurrections and resistance to government by disarming the people is oftener meant than avowed by [those wishing to institute gun control].[8]

The liberal establishment (more appropriately referred to as postmodernists or neo-Marxists) claims that the Second Amendment protection is meant only for the militia. Therefore, according to liberals, the only people protected by the Second Amendment would be National Guardsmen. They make this absurd claim without ever defining what was meant by "the militia." George Mason, the co-author of the Second Amendment, described the militia thusly: "...a well-regulated Militia, composed of the Gentlemen, Freeholders, and other Freemen was necessary to protect our ancient laws and liberty from the standing army...."[9] It is clear that he was not referring to a standing military organization

---

6   See, Kennedy & Kennedy, **Only Empires are Indivisible**, Chapter 10, *The South Was Right!* 3rd edition (Shotwell Publishing, Columbia, SC: 2020), 259-266.

7   *The Anti-Federalist: The Address and Reasons of Dissent of the Minority of the Convention of Pennsylvania To Their Constituents,* Herbert J. Storing Ed. (Chicago and London: The University of Chicago Press: 1992), 207.

8   Rawle, William, *A View of the Constitution of the United States: Secession as Taught at West Point* 2nd edition, Kennedy & Kennedy editors (The Scuppernong Press, Wake Forest, NC: 2020), 97.

9   George Mason as cited in, LaPierre, Wayne, *Guns, Crime, and Freedom* (Regnery Publishing, Inc., Washington, DC: 1994), 5.

Patrick Henry knew that freedom loving Americans would not allow the British to disarm free men.

such as the National Guard but to free citizens—in short, the people who possess private weapons of their own. Thomas Jefferson wrote in the Virginia Constitution that "...no free man shall be debarred the use of arms within his own land." George Mason left no doubt as to why it is important to maintain the citizen's right to keep and bear arms: "To disarm the people [is] the best and most effectual way to enslave them." Contemporary Americans need to be reminded that it was Britain's attempt to disarm the Colonists that led to the battle at Lexington and the "shot heard around the world."

Our Colonial Forefathers did not insist upon the Second Amendment so that modern day Americans could go squirrel hunting. Sports shooting and hunting had nothing to do with the adoption of the Second Amendment. Defending our civil liberties against tyrants was the primary motivating factor. Tyrants will not tolerate an armed people—an armed people will not tolerate a tyrant!

The value of private arms in the hands of free men was well proven during the Revolutionary War with Great Britain. One British politician noted that the American people were dangerous because "...with principles of right in their minds and hearts, and with arms in their hands [Americans were determined] to assert those principles."[10] The British Empire knew that dangers posed by armed freemen and attempted their own version of "assault weapons" control, an attempt that led to the Battle of Lexington and the "shot heard around the world."

> On October 19, 1774, Lord Dartmouth, in a circular letter to the Colonial Governors, informed them that the King, by an order in Council, had prohibited the exportation from Great Britain of gun powder; or any sort of arms or ammunition, and his Lordship required the Governors to prevent the importation of the prohibited articles into the several colonies. Not content with preventing the purchase by the colonies of the munitions of war, the next move was to seize and carry away, or destroy, the ammunition in their possession.[11]

Patrick Henry, as usual, saw to the core of the issue. He told his fellow Virginians that the issue of American independence would not become a burning issue in the hearts of Americans because of the tax on tea and other provocations:

> But tell them of the robbery of the magazine, and that the next step will be to disarm them, and they will be then ready to fly to arms to defend themselves.[12]

During the War for Southern Independence, the people of New Orleans found out what it was like to live under the heel of a tyrant. After the occupation of New Orleans by federal forces under the command of Yankee General Benjamin "Beast" Butler, the city was placed under martial law. The agents of martial law were so oppressive that they even hung (lynched) a young man because he pulled down the invader's flag *before* the city had

---

10 Chatham, Member of Parliament, as cited in, Henry, William Wirt, editor *Patrick Henry: Life, Correspondence, and Speeches* (1981, Sprinkle Publications, Harrisonburg, VA: 1993), I, 272.

11 Henry, 276.

12 Henry, 276.

Post War Photo
Holt Collier. Former CSA Sharp-
shooter

formally surrendered. All civil liberties were restricted, including freedom of religion, freedom of speech, and freedom of assembly; and, of course, an order was given by Butler to confiscate all guns held by private citizens.[13] During Butler's reign of terror, millions of dollars of private property were stolen (confiscated from "rebels") from the people of Louisiana and sent up North—much for Butler's private collection. Thieves and tyrants know that it is much safer to rob unarmed people. Any country that has been invaded understands how important it is to have free men who possess and know how to use firearms.

A great example of the benefit of guns in the hands of citizens is provided by the story of one of America's first black sharpshooter. Holt Collier was born a slave in Mississippi. His master gave him a gun and told him to develop his hunting skills and provide meat for the newly established plantation. He became such a good shot that it was said that he killed more bears than Daniel Boone and Davy Crocket combined. Holt Collier joined the Ninth Texas Cavalry, CSA, during the War for Southern Independence. Skilled hunters are ideal material for the creation of an efficient military.

Confederate General Nathan Bedford Forrest used local citizens armed with their own weapons to help him defeat Yankee General Streight. Streight's army outnumbered Forrest's army but that did not stop Forrest. Streight was running as fast as he could trying to put distance between him and Forrest. Streight's aim was to seize Rome, Georgia. Forrest sent a local mailman on an eighteen-mile Paul Revere ride shouting "the Yankees are coming" as he rode toward Rome, Georgia. Soon church bells began to ring in the middle of the night. Forrest sent this message to the citizens

---

13   Winters, John D., *The Civil War in Louisiana* (Louisiana University Press, Baton Rouge, LA: 1963), 136.

of Rome, Georgia, "Prepare your selves to repulse them—they (Yankees) have two Mountain howitzers. I will be close on them. I have killed three hundred of their men. They are running for their lives." The local militia was joined by dozens of local old men and young boys armed with shotguns and hunting rifles. When Yankee General Streight found Rome, Georgia, prepared, its citizens ready to defend their city, and with Forrest now closing in on him—surrender was the only option.[14] These three cases taken for the history of the War for Southern Independence demonstrate, in the New Orleans example, the natural fear that tyrants have for an armed citizenry, Holt Collier's case demonstrates the value of free citizens who are familiar with outdoor living and the use of firearms, and, in the Rome, Georgia, example, the importance of arms in the hands of private citizens. This is why our neo-Marxist enemies are so fearful of armed, law-abiding, Americans. They are not worried about the criminals roaming the streets in inner city America—they are fearful of armed law-abiding Americans who are ready to defend their natural rights as free people.

General N.B. Forrest, CSA

---

14 Mitcham, Jr., Samuel W., *Bust Hell Wide Open-the life of Nathan Bedford Forrest* (Regnery History, Washington, DC: 2016), 114.

Chapter 5

TYRANTS WILL NOT ALLOW THEIR SUBJECTS TO KEEP AND BEAR ARMS

ADOLPH HITLER, the archetypical tyrant of the twentieth century, was a believer in gun control. In 1938, Hitler signed a Nazi gun-control law for the federal government of Germany. This was done after he had consolidated power from the German states into a strong central government in Berlin. His gun-control law required police permission to own a pistol. All firearms were required to be registered. Those who wanted to "keep and bear" arms were instructed to join the army. The Nazis also enacted special gun-control laws for those we would today call "politically incorrect" individuals. Shortly thereafter, the gas chambers began working overtime. No guns—no resistance.

Firearms registration lists were used by the Nazi SS to collect weapons from political enemies and occasionally to collect the owner as well! Once again, just so you will understand our point, TYRANTS DO NOT LIKE ARMED CITIZENS. Neo-Marxists do not like the fact that American-values voters are highly armed. That is why they are incessantly pushing for more gun control legislation. Their aim is not the gun but to increase their ability to control "We the people." In reality it is not gun control the neo-Marxists are after—it is people control.

How can "We the people" protect our Second Amendment rights? The same way we can protect all of our rights and liberties. We must have a strong political force organized within each state to protect our rights within our state and to serve as a counterbalance to an aggressive federal government. As James Madison declared:

> ... State governments, with the people on their side, would be able to repel the danger [of an oppressive federal government] ... Besides the advantage of being armed, which the Americans possess over the people of almost every other nation, the existence of subordinate governments [sovereign states], to which the people are attached, and by which the militia officers are appointed, forms a barrier against the enterprise of ambition...[1]

When the rights and liberties of "We the people" of the sovereign states are infringed upon by an abusive Federal government, it is the duty of the sovereign state to be the protector of our rights and liberties. This is what our Founding Fathers intended.[2] When the Federal government attempts to compel the local authorities to enforce unconstitutional gun-control laws, then it is the duty of the sovereign state to stand between the local official and the unconstitutional federal law, court order, Executive Order, rule or regulation.

"We the people" must not rely upon electing "good" conservatives to Congress because, as we have witnessed, they do not always remain "good" once they obtain office. We must not rely upon the chance of electing a "conservative" president who will veto laws that infringe upon our Second Amendment rights. We cannot entrust our constitutional liberties to the rulings of five or more elitists, unelected, Supreme Court Justices. No! Freedom and liberty are best served and protected at the local level by "We the

---

1   Madison, James, *The Federalist No. 46.*

2   See Kentucky and Virginia Resolutions of 1798 passed by these state legislatures and written by Thomas Jefferson and James Madison in: Kennedy & Kennedy, *The South Was Right!* 3rd edition, 230-2.

people" within our sovereign state. A government that desires to disarm law-abiding citizens is evil enough to take away all the rest of our rights under the Constitution. The enemy that wants to abolish your right to keep and bear arms is the same neo-Marxist enemy that removed prayer and Bible reading from "our" schools, that rejected the four-thousand-year-old Biblical definition of marriage as being between one man and one woman, and the same neo-Marxist ruling elite that made transgenders a federally protected minority. Our neo-Marxist enemy is the avowed enemy of Western Christian civilization. We must defeat them on all fronts. To defeat such a well-financed and entrenched enemy we must take away their source of political power. The primary source of their power is the supreme Federal government. We can do this by setting in motion a movement composed of American-values voters in Red State, Red County America. This movement will be the force that compels the ruling elites to recognize our rights under the Constitution. Together with fellow conservatives across Red State and Red County America we shall restore America's original, Constitutionally-limited, Republic of Sovereign States—a country of our own where the protections inscribed in the Constitution are enforced via real States' Rights inclusive of the rights of nullification and secession.

Chapter 6

SECURING 2ND AMENDMENT RIGHTS VIA NULLIFICATION & SECESSION

SECESSION AND NULLIFICATION are unalienable rights reserved to "We the people" in the Constitution.[1] But some may think that in such an ideologically diverse America such ideas would be impossible to implement. Some may wonder, "What would happen to neo-Marxist voters in large urban areas within a Red State when our Sovereign State Constitutional Amendment is ratified?"[2] Unlike our neo-Marxist enemies we believe that people have a right to live under a government that supports their values and interests—even if we do not agree with their beliefs and ideology. How would nullification or secession work in the real world? Take the State of Georgia for example. If Georgia decides to nullify *Roe v Wade* but the people of Atlanta wanted to keep abortion legal in their city, then Atlanta could declare itself a city-state. But that would mean that no state funds would be going to assist the city-state. It would also mean that the concept of "probable cause" would no longer

---

1 These essential American rights existed prior to the Constitution and was boldly proclaimed in the July 4th 1776 Declaration of Independence. It is one of the unnumberable unnamed rights reserved in the Ninth and Tenth Amendments of the U.S. Constitution. Remember, the Constitution is not a list of all rights belonging to the people but an outline for the formation of the federal government and the specific duties the Sovereign States delegated to the federal government. Note: Delegated not surrendered to the federal government.

2 Copy of our Sovereign State U.S. Constitutional Amendment in Chapter 12.

apply to Atlanta citizens when they leave their city-state and come into Georgia. They would be subject to stop and search by Georgia law enforcement. The state may decide to set up facial recognition cameras to profile known gang members and felons leaving Atlanta and coming into Georgia.

In a similar vein, if the State of Georgia decides to enact non-arbitrary voting qualifications that would not allow welfare recipients or felons to vote, but Atlanta's people, while objecting to these new qualifications for voting, they do not want to secede from Georgia, then the city—as opposed to a seceded city-state—of Atlanta could enact their own voting qualifications for city elections. But any elections pertaining to matters of the state, such as statewide offices or ballot initiatives—in those cases only state qualified voters would be allowed to participate in such elections. Or suppose a section of Atlanta, or any American city dominated by neo-Marxist Democrats, decides that it has had enough of neo-Marxist rule. The people within a designated section of Atlanta could petition the State of Georgia for a new city charter for their section of Atlanta and thereby secede from the neo-Marxist controlled part of Atlanta. Such a move has already been suggested by the affluent Buckhead area of Atlanta.[3]

SECESSION IN CONTEMPORARY AMERICA

Contemporary, 2020, discussion about secession is not new in America.[4] In a best-selling book *The South Was Right!* (2nd edition 1994—3rd edition published in 2020) argued that the South had the same moral and legal right to independence and self-government in 1861 as the American Colonies had in 1776. Recall that all thirteen colonies were slave holding colonies in 1776, yet slavery and the

---

3   https://www.breitbart.com/crime/2021/06/18/atlanta-community-moves-separate-city-rising-crime-divorce-final/ accessed 6/20/2021.

4   Even a Roman Catholic from New Hampshire in December 2020, suggested secession in an article titled **The Catholic Case for Secession?** https://www.crisismagazine.com/2020/the-catholic-case-for-secession?fbclid=IwAR3C8GBnBMpv BO4c_ZSAZILqLrglvxrry3TzW6DLZGxj7iP5sDNlU2L3SzY#.X-f1QpXY9Lo.facebook accessed 12/27/2020.

New England states participation in the slave trade did not nullify the Colonies' right to self-government. In 2017 *Dixie Rising-Rules for Rebels* was published (2nd edition in 2021) in which the author urged the creation of Provisional State governments[5] that would conduct irregular *political* warfare for the purpose of reclaiming America's original Constitutionally-limited Republic of Sovereign States by passing a proposed Sovereign State Amendment. But, if the Blue states and the neo-Marxists who control the Deep State reject our Constitutional Amendment, then it would trigger the secession of Southern States plus any other American-values state or county that wanted to join the South as we recreate a Constitutionally-limited Republic of Sovereign States—a nation of our own.

Shortly after Trump's election in 2016 there arose a Calexit movement urging the secession of liberal California from the U.S.A. Prior to the 2020 election there arose a movement in several counties in Oregon, California, and Nevada to secede from their states and form another state or join Idaho. The establishing of "sanctuary cities" in liberal dominated areas is actually a contemporary endorsement of nullification—the right of people at the local level to ignore federal laws that the people find objectionable. While liberals strongly support this form of nullification (which is one step removed from secession), they would quickly send the federal marshals to any conservative state that attempted to nullify partial-birth abortion, nullify the use of taxpayer-funded welfare to illegal aliens, or nullify federal gun control laws. Blue state people can nullify laws they do not agree with because they have a country of their own—*they are not a stateless people.* Red State and Red

---

5   Provisional government: An organized group of individuals holding traditional, conservative, political, and moral values who work together to bring political pressure on elected officials to encourage them to protect and promote traditional, American values. It also uses various forms of public information to educate the public about the necessity of standing firm against America's neo-Marxist enemies. It serves as the counter-balance to the evil, politically correct, leftist, shadow government that currently controls America, while working for a fundamental change in the way in which "We the people" control our Federal government via the ratification of our Sovereign State Amendment or creating a new and independent nation of our own via Red State-Red County secession.

County people have no government dedicated to protecting and promoting their interests and values—today *Red State and Red County people are a stateless people.*

As far as Blue State folks are concerned, the function of bitter-clingers, smelly Walmart shoppers, irredeemables, and deplorables (this is the neo-Marxist definition of conservative American-values voters) is to: (1) Provide tax revenues to finance the supreme Federal government and the neo-Marxist indoctrination centers masquerading as schools and universities; (2) provide our sons and daughters to serve as cannon fodder in the endless wars that benefit those with close connection to the Deep State's military-industrial complex; and, (3) we must meekly submit our children to neo-Marxist indoctrination in Critical Race Theory, gun control, LGBTQ rights etc., in public schools and universities. Simply put, our function in present-day, politically correct America is to hear and obey—this, of course, is the function of political slaves. And "We the people," under the current neo-Marxist political system, are political slaves!

SECESSION—
A LONG HELD AMERICAN POLITICAL PRINCIPLE

The United States of America was founded via an act of secession from the British Empire in 1776. Secession is not new or something dreamed-up by Southerners in 1861. Representatives from New England threatened to secede if Louisiana was admitted to the Union and voiced the threat of secession again when Texas was applying for admission to the Union. Note that by accepting the Sovereign nation of Texas into the Union as a Sovereign State, the United States recognized as legitimate Texas' secession from Mexico in 1836. Secession is a very important American political principle. Free people have the unalienable right to secede from an oppressive government but stateless people have no such right—stateless people are political slaves to the political establishment that rules over them. Unfortunately, too many Americans do not realize that "We the people" are a stateless people.

Perhaps the two best recent examples of Americans being a stateless people is shown in the Federal Court overturning the vote of American-values voters in California. In 2008 the voters in California voted overwhelmingly in favor of a ballot initiative declaring marriage as between one man and one woman. This definition is a traditional Judeo-Christian definition of marriage that dates back over 4000 years. Yet, the Federal Court stepped in and nullified the democratically expressed will of the people. In another California ballot initiative, the people of California voted to prohibit the use of taxpayer funds to provide welfare to illegal aliens. The people spoke, they voted and passed the ballot initiative, but once again, the Federal government stepped in and nullified the will of "We the people" of that once sovereign state. "We the people" in Red-States and Red Counties who hold traditional, American values are in fact a stateless people. We have no government to protect and promote our values and interests—we need to re-create America's original Constitutionally-limited Republic of Sovereign States or, if necessary, create a nation of our own!

Another example of how even "conservative" Republican controlled legislatures do the bidding of their neo-Marxist masters in Washington, DC, is when the legislature of Mississippi nullified the expressed will of Mississippi's people. The people, in a special ballot initiative, voted overwhelmingly to keep their traditional flag. Republicans in the state legislature, and the Republican governor, nullified the will of the people. In a rogue session, specially designed to overthrow the will of the people, the "special" session voted and the governor then signed a bill to replace the state's flag. The majority of Mississippi's citizens are in fact stateless—they have no political entity, Republican or Democrat, to protect and promote their interest. The existing state government, elected by these same people, is nothing more than America's ruling elite's puppet government. As a puppet government it obediently did the will of its master—the ruling elite and its politically correct shadow government.[6] This is true not only for the people of Mississippi but for all Southerners and all conservative, God-fearing, folks residing in what neo-Marxists refer to as "Podunk U.S.A."

In the past we have placed our political hope on electing "good" conservatives. Unfortunately, this has done little to defeat the neo-Marxists who are determined to disarm law-abiding Americans. In reality these "good" conservatives were actually counterfeit conservatives who used American-values voters to get elected. They are "counterfeit conservatives" because during the past one hundred years of the "conservative movement," conservatives have not conserved anything! Conservatives have stood by as liberals/ progressives (they are all neo-Marxists) slowly destroyed the very fabric of our Constitutionally-limited Republic of Sovereign States. Counterfeit conservatives have offered no effective alternative to the insidious efforts of the left to destroy America's moral and constitutional standards. Today's politically correct, neo-Marxist America is damning evidence of one hundred years of conservative failure. At best conservatives have been a place holder for the left, giving the appearance of being an opposition party. Reactionary, counterfeit conservatives are not psychologically or motivationally equipped to defeat America's neo-Marxist enemies. Reactionary, timid, counterfeit conservatives will not restore Constitutional liberty to America—we need American-values revolutionaries willing to engage the enemy in irregular political warfare. Otherwise, we will remain a stateless people, subjugated to the increasingly belligerent will of America's neo-Marxist ruling elite.

Because "We the people" of America's Red States and Red Counties do not have a "state" (nation) to protect our interests we have been reduced to the level of a stateless people. We have allowed ourselves to become the political slaves to America's neo-Marxist, ruling elites in the Deep State, Wall Street, and Silicon

---

6 America's politically correct society is governed by an evil, leftist, shadow government that establishes its immoral, neo-Marxist ideology as the new standard of American social/political conduct. This evil shadow government consists of postmodernists in academia, the mainline and digital media, the entertainment industry, establishment politicians, Deep State bureaucrats, financial and Globalists elites. They are left-of-center ideologues united in their determination to destroy traditional America and Western Christian civilization and make a huge profit in the process.

Valley. Our First and Second Amendment rights, once protected by the Constitution, have been reduced to privileges that we are allowed to exercise when and only when it is approved by our political masters. If we dare to protest, we are subjected to what Justice Clarence Thomas described as a mainline media promoted high-tech lynch mob.

The neo-Marxist, shadow government's ministry of propaganda—the mainline media, digital media, and the entertainment industry (especially Hollywood)—will subject conservatives who dare to oppose efforts to destroy our Second Amendment rights to unending and slanderous personal attacks. Neo-Marxists are experts in using character assassination to silence conservative opposition. A recent (2020) national poll discovered that conservatives by a margin of over 75% self-censor to avoid being personally and slanderously attacked by leftists. Without realizing it, we have allowed America's evil, neo-Marxist, shadow government to nullify the First Amendment's right of free speech, free expression, and, during the Communist Chinese COVID outbreak, freedom of religion. Our neo-Marxist enemies ignore truth, facts and civil discussion—the only thing that matters to the neo-Marxist ministry of propaganda is that they silence and destroy anyone who would dare to question their leftist ideology. If we are to survive, we must have a nation of our own. We must reclaim America's original, Constitutionally-limited, Republic of Sovereign States or create a nation of our own. Only political power can counter political oppression.

RECENT STATE & COUNTY ATTEMPTS TO NULLIFY FEDERAL GUN CONTROL—WILL IT WORK?

A number of states and counties have enacted laws and ordinances which, in effect, make their state or county a Second Amendment gun rights sanctuary state or county. They are following the example of neo-Marxist States and cities that refuse to enforce national immigration laws by making their cities "sanctuary cities." This has been very effective for the neo-Marxists but, under the current political system, will it be as effective for American-values, conservative states and counties?

The April 7, 2021, issue of the Epoch Times reported that Arizona recently passed, and the Governor signed, a law that makes Arizona a Second Amendment sanctuary state. Another conservative publication, The New American, reported that the Governor of Iowa also signed a state law making Iowa a Second Amendment sanctuary state. As of April, 2021, Iowa became the 19th state to pass such laws. [7]

The major problem with such laws, enacted by conservatives, is that, unlike sanctuary city immigration laws enacted by neo-Marxist states and cities, conservatives have no government to protect our right to enact such laws—laws which are an example of state nullification under America's original Constitution.[8] Conservatives are a stateless people. We have no government to protect and promote our interests. We live under the rule of a neo-Marxist supreme federal government that will oppress and infringe our legitimate rights under the *original* Constitution. The neo-Marxist political establishment will not hesitate to send in federal marshals or federal troops to arrest any Red State or Red County elected official who refuses to implement federal gun-control legislation. Our freedoms and liberty are at risk as long as "We the people" allow the unconstitutional and illegitimate supreme Federal government to remain in power. The question is how do we obtain the power to defeat the neo-Marxist, shadow government and its ruling elite in Washington, DC?

---

7   As reported by Benson, Al Jr., April 13, 2021 at: https://revisedhistory.wordpress. com/ accessed 4/19/2021.

8   For a list and description of nine sovereign states that nullified federal laws and even a portion of the Constitution, see, Kennedy, James Ronald, *Be Ye Separate: Bible Belt Revival or Marxist Revolution* (Xulon Press, Maitland, FL: 2021), 9-15.

Chapter 7

MAKING AN END-RUN AROUND THE POLITICAL ESTABLISHMENT

THE POLITICAL STATUS QUO—also known as the Deep State or the Swamp—is designed to operate around election cycles with power concentrated in faraway Washington, DC. Our *strategic* battle plan is to do an "end run around" or "outflank" their battle plan! The political establishment works for the benefit of the ruling elite. The current system of political control is designed to assure the survival of the current political establishment by favoring incumbency. A *fundamental* change in the current system of political rule in America will never occur if we continue to engage in traditional political campaigns—business-as-usual politics. The current system of American government is not only corrupted, it is also corrupting. It corrupts even "good" people once they are elected into the most exclusive club in America—the ruling elite in Washington, DC. We propose a Red State-Red County Revolution as the only way to *fundamentally* change the status quo and return power to "We the people" within our sovereign states and local communities. We will move governmental power over our lives and communities from Washington, DC, and return it to "We the people" within our Sovereign States. This is the only solution to the unconstitutional rule of America's self-anointed elite—an elite backed by an evil, neo-Marxist, shadow government that now controls America's institutions of social and political influence.

Feeble, ineffective, conservative efforts of the past brought us to this point—continuing the same feeble efforts will never bring about victory but it will assure the total destruction of American liberty. If we fail to take decisive action today, the little upon which we now barely subsist will be taken from us!

The past one hundred years of failed conservative efforts has taught us that if we keep doing the same things we have always done, then we will get the same results! The same results being a politically correct nation controlled by a neo-Marxist, shadow government. A leftist nation with more taxes, more federal regulations, more intrusive federal court decisions, more inflation, less personal privacy, fewer personal liberties, fewer property rights, eventual draconian anti-gun laws, and worst of all, *more demoralizing conservative failures!* The lesson we must take away from the past one hundred years of conservative failure is that the political status quo is designed to favor those who want to maintain (Republicans) or expand (Democrats) a big, centralized, oppressive, supreme federal government.[1] In America's business-as-usual political arena, the rules of engagement are set by those who have a vested interest in maintaining "We the people" in a subservient position as political slaves of America's ruling elite. As political slaves, we have little or no way of effectively resisting our masters in faraway Washington, DC. We are indeed a stateless people under the rule of a neo-Marxist, shadow government. We shall remain a stateless people unless we take immediate action to reclaim America's original, Constitutionally-limited Republic of Sovereign States or, if necessary, establish an independent nation of our own.

---

1   The term "supreme Federal government" is used to draw a distinction between America's original and *legitimate* Constitutionally-limited Republic of Sovereign States and today's *illegitimate*, supreme Federal government. In America's original government "We the people" within our state(s) exercised the ultimate control over the federal government but in today's supreme Federal government, the Federal government decides for itself what limits, if any, are imposed by the Constitution upon Federal governmental powers. This is a radical and unconstitutional departure from America's Founding Fathers original intentions.

Once conservatives realize that politics as usual only plays into the hands of those who want to exploit us, then we can begin the efforts that will ultimately produce a strategic victory.

America's ruling elite realize that in a "democracy" the best way to maintain control over those who pay for the cost of government—the productive citizens—is to allow productive taxpayers to enjoy the *illusion* that they, the productive subjects, somehow have a say in the political system. Middle-class taxpayers pay for the political establishment that exploits so much of the productive subject's income for the benefit of the government's parasitic elements—apparently all done in the most democratic manner. These government parasites always bloc vote for the liberal, Democrat candidate. Just to be clear, let me point out that the Federal government's parasitic elements consist of the ruling elite, corporate welfare recipients, social welfare recipients, and Globalists. They are branded "parasites" because, as is the case of politicians and social welfare recipients, they produce nothing of value that would be demanded in an unhampered free market. Corporate welfare recipients' relationship with government allows crony capitalist to gain "profits" that they would not have gained in the free market. The special privileges granted to Silicon Valley's digital monopolist (Facebook, Google, Twitter, etc.) is an excellent example of the supreme Federal government granting favors to its neo-Marxist allies.

The ruling elite know how important it is to keep political slaves quiet and docile! Allowing a few insignificant electoral victories every now and then is a very effective way to allow "We the people" to "let off a little steam" without endangering the political status quo. And remember, the political status quo is very profitable for both Republican and Democrat ruling elites. American-values voters must understand that a few tactical political victories here and there will never produce the *fundamental* change needed if our rights under the Constitution are to be secure—safe from federal encroachments.

America's current political establishment is designed around election cycles. Vast amounts of energy and resources (especially money) are available to the political establishment. These resources will be marshaled each election cycle to assure no one is elected who might endanger the existence of the ruling elite's Deep State in Washington, DC. At best the ruling elite and their shadow government will allow a few Republican (conservative in name only i.e., counterfeit conservative) victories, but these "victories" are mere window dressing—not a sincere effort to *fundamentally* change the nature of the illegitimate, unconstitutional, supreme Federal government. America's elected conservative office holders have never initiated an earnest effort to replace the supreme Federal government with a Constitutionally-limited Republic of Sovereign States. They have never had the courage to insist upon a new Republic in which the protections declared in the original Constitution are enforced by "We the people" via real States' Rights—real States' Rights including the rights of state nullification and secession.

Business-as-usual politicians have no real desire to replace the current supreme Federal government with a federal government modeled upon the government created by our Founding Fathers. If an "outsider" is elected (such as Trump for example), the neo-Marxist, shadow government will wage an unrelenting war against the outsider and eventually drive him from office. Justice Clarence Thomas referred to this as a high-tech lynch mob using character assassination to silence and eventually drive conservatives from office. Once the neo-Marxist, shadow government drives the conservative from office, they will then replace the "outsider" with an individual with strong connections and loyalty to the Washington, DC, establishment, someone willing to work with the Swamp, the Deep State, and Washington's political establishment.

Once conservatives realize that politics as usual only plays into the hands of those who want to exploit us, once we realize that electing "good" conservatives will not produce a *fundamental* change in the current supreme Federal government, then we can begin the efforts that will ultimately produce a strategic victory—a victory that will destroy the evil, neo-Marxist, shadow government and remove the political ruling elite from their haughty positions of perks, privileges, and power. "We the people" will replace the political establishment with a nation of our own, a nation governed on the principles of America's original Constitutional Republic of Sovereign States.

Christian conservatives who object to the abortion decision of *Roe v. Wade* think that all they need to do is to pass a constitutional amendment overruling the court's decision. But an amendment without some effective political force to enforce it would be meaningless—having no more power than America's immigration laws have in Blue States. For example, gun owners have the Second Amendment that plainly declares the right to keep and bear arms, but that has not stopped the ruling elite, at the federal, state, and local level, from constantly attacking this vital Constitutional right. In the recent (2020) riots, neo-Marxist city officials arrested a husband and wife who used, but did not fire, legally owned weapons to protect their home—so much for the vaunted right to keep and bear arms! A constitutional amendment without an effective political entity to enforce that right is useless. Even if Christian conservatives could enact their favored amendment, it would prove no more useful to them than the Ninth and Tenth Amendments have been for advocates of real States' Rights and eventually the Second Amendment for those of us who want to preserve our right to keep and bear arms. Without the benefit of the sovereign state "We the people" are a stateless people. Constitutional liberty will never be secure **if** we allow the supreme Federal government to continue dominating the sovereign states.[2] But the sovereign state needs more than business-as-usual politicians running the state. We will need statesmen governing our states. Men who understand that the first function of the sovereign state is to protect the rights reserved in the Constitution to "We the people" of the sovereign states. We need courageous leaders who will use the sovereign state and its ability to interpose its sovereign authority between its citizens and an aggressive and abusive Federal government. Otherwise, we will never be protected from an abusive and tyrannical Federal government. The only way to reclaim state sovereignty is by the states ratifying our Sovereign State Amendment or, if necessary, the secession of Red States and Counties and the creation of a nation of our own.

Our goal must be to present the political establishment with a social/political battle they have never faced, one they are ill-equipped to defend against and one that allows "We the people" to leverage our strength at the local (grassroots) level. Think of the effort to ratify our Sovereign State Amendment as our effort to outflank (or make an end run around) the political wing of the ruling elite's army, while our efforts to educate and motivate "We the people" at the local level is our effort to outflank the politically correct, neo-Marxist ministry of propaganda wing of the ruling elite's army. Working with fellow believers in liberty (traditional Christians, Southern heritage champions, Tea Party folks, etc.), folks who are determined not to repeat the mistakes committed by conservatives for the past one-hundred-years, together we will form a movement that will restore America's original Constitutionally-limited Republic of Sovereign States. But, if folks in Blue States

---

2   In 1787-8, States such as New York and Virginia included, in their ratification of the Constitution, the condition that the states retained the right to recall any or all of its delegated powers if the people of the state deemed it necessary. Such right, the right to recall delegated rights, i.e., secede from an established government as the Thirteen Colonies did in 1776, is but one of the constitutionally protected unenumerated, unalienable, rights protected via the Ninth Amendment. The right to determine when human life begins is an example of an unenumerated right that belongs (exclusively) to "We the people" of the Sovereign States. In 1798 Thomas Jefferson and James Madison writing the Kentucky and Virginia Resolutions plainly announced and described the States' Right to take any measure it deemed necessary to protect the citizens of a sovereign state from oppressive acts of the Federal government.

and the neo-Marxists who control the Deep State reject our efforts to restore America's legitimate government, then we shall create a Red State-Red County nation of our own!

For the past century or more conservatives have "talked" about conserving something. It is impossible to determine what these spinless conservatives were trying to conserve other than their political status quo. While elected "conservatives" talked, "We the people" watched the Federal government morph into what it is today—a supreme, centralized Federal government, with a neo-Marxist, ruling elite who use the political establishment to exploit productive, taxpaying, subjects. "Subjects" because "We the people" are no longer free citizens who control "our" government. *The current government functions for the benefit of the ruling elite and those with close connections to the ruling elite.* But again, it must be stressed that our movement is dedicated to peaceful social and political action—our money, time, and emotional energy must be used to produce measurable results for the exclusive benefit of "We the people." We will use our time, money, and energy to gain a strategic victory that will produce a society in which "We the people" will be secure in our rights, liberty, and property. We will re-create a nation in which Constitutional rights are secure and protected by "We the people" in our Sovereign States. We shall re-create a Constitutionally-limited U.S.A. or, if necessary, we shall create a nation of our own. One way or another—our liberty, our Constitutional rights, our freedom shall be secured! Our tenure as the left's political slaves will end when we have a government of our own—we will then no longer be a stateless people!

The strategic goal is to present to the current political ruling elite a battle they have never before faced, a battle designed to favor our strength and to capitalize on their weakness. It will not be a traditional political campaign—that would be playing to their strength. Why? The political establishment is designed and structured in a fashion to guarantee its continuation by assuring incumbency for those politicians who favor maintaining the political status quo and defeating or corrupting "good" conservatives.

If a "good" conservative is elected the political establishment works overtime to turn the "good" conservative into a counterfeit conservative or guarantee his defeat in the next election cycle.

Enfeebled, counterfeit conservatives may choose to continue the same political efforts they have always used and in so doing, no doubt, gain a few impressive tactical victories, but with each election cycle conservative "victories" are fewer. In the long run the machinery of big government (the supreme Federal government) will always be in place ready to churn out more intrusive, politically correct, federalism as soon as counterfeit conservatives once again self-destruct and return control back to America's left-of-center, neo-Marxist ruling elite.[3]

Why not win one strategic victory and change the status quo forever!

---

3 See, **How Not To Win**, Introduction, Kennedy, James Ronald, *Dixie Rising Rules for Rebels* 2nd edition, vii-xii.

Chapter 8

HANGING THE POLITICAL ELITES ON THE HORNS OF A DILEMMA

CONSERVATIVES BELIEVE that government is, in and of itself, dangerous to human liberty. Therefore, government must be limited. The only way to limit the current supreme Federal government is to hang the political establishment on the horns of a dilemma: Either they pass our Sovereign State Constitutional Amendment (Chapter 12 has complete copy of this amendment) which will re-establish the American principle of real States' Rights or the neo-Marxist political establishment will be faced with Americans in Red States and Red Counties initiating a secession movement. They will be faced with the embarrassing situation of explaining to the world why half of "their" nation's subjects no longer want to be part of "their" government.

Our proposed Sovereign State Amendment acknowledges the right of "We the people" via our sovereign state to nullify unconstitutional federal acts or, if necessary, to secede from an oppressive Federal government. With this amendment in place any act by the Federal government that "We the people" within our sovereign state feel to be unconstitutional can be immediately halted! For example, instead of wasting time and money trying to elect "good" conservatives (who for reasons already explained do not always remain "good" once elected) or protecting Second

Amendment rights or fighting for the right of the state to protect the lives of its unborn citizens—all good fights but fights we have no chance of permanently winning—we change the entire political system to one that favors "We the people." Instead of wearing ourselves out fighting good tactical battles—why not win one strategic victory by creating a mass movement demanding the passage of our Sovereign State Amendment or else "We the people" will create a nation of our own. This valid threat of secession and, *if necessary*, the actual act of secession, will change America's political establishment forever! The Deep State swamp will be drained of its ability to dominate "We the people."

Washington, DC's political establishment is designed to maintain a system of government in which the ruling elite and those with close connections to the ruling elite prosper at the expense of the average taxpaying American.[1] "We the people" have become America's forgotten man, the one who pays the bills but has no effective way to control "his" government! We have become political slaves to the ruling political establishment. The political status quo works for the benefit of the ruling elite. The current system of political control is designed to assure the survival of the status quo and favor the re-election of those politicians who are loyal to the Washington, DC, Deep State. This is NOT the government our Founding Fathers crafted. This is NOT the legitimate Federal government the Sovereign States ratified! It is an *illegitimate* government far removed from the legitimate Federal government designed by the Founding Fathers and given its political life when the Sovereign States ratified the original Constitution.

If "We the people" are to regain our status as free citizens in a Constitutionally-limited Republic of Sovereign States, then a *fundamental* change in the current system of political rule in America must transpire. If "We the people" fail to act, then the little liberty that we are now allowed to enjoy—especially our Second Amendment rights—will be taken from us. The complete

---

1 President Eisenhower called it the "military industrial complex." But in the modern-day Deep State it is much larger. It includes quasi-monopolistic, digital-media, companies in Silicon Valley, postmodernists in academia, the mainline media, the Federal Reserve, and Globalists—just to name a few.

destruction of Constitutional liberty will occur in our lifetime, if we continue to engage in traditional, business-as-usual political campaigns.

The important thing for "We the people" to recognize is that America's political establishment is designed to serve society's parasitic elements by exploiting society's productive element under the euphemism of "redistributing wealth," "equity," and "social justice." As long as "We the people" play by the rules established by the ruling elite, and refereed by their paid judges, we will always lose! The ruling elite have designed a system that encourages and facilitates the development of neo-Marxist voting blocs. The ruling elite use wealth extorted from productive citizens to reward the parasitic elements for voting for left-wing, liberal, and socialist, political candidates.[2]

Expanding the role of government is the primary function of the Democratic wing of the political status quo, while the Republican wing is responsible for maintaining the status quo by keeping "conservatives" docile, pacified, and politically harmless (impotent is a better description). Republican office holders and officials within the Washington, DC, Beltway, state-elected Republican officials yearning to join the exclusive club in Washington, and the

Both liberal Democrat and conservative Republican politicians and party bosses have a vested interest in preserving the political status quo.

---

2   Regardless of what name they may be identified by, they are all (figuratively) part of the same postmodernist tribe. Whether liberal, progressive, secular humanist, neo-Marxist, each is a clan within the same tribe. As clans often do, they may disagree among themselves but all leftwing "clans" are united in their effort to destroy Christian-based Western civilization. These leftist clans or groups make-up America's politically correct neo-Marxist shadow government.

Republican state/national party leadership all serve to provide cover for Democrats who are actively expanding the role and scope of the supreme Federal government. Republicans provide cover by providing the mirage of being the opposition party! In reality they only oppose the efforts of the Democrats to control the reins of federal power. Republicans do not oppose the concept of an all-powerful, supreme Federal government (the *illegitimate* political status quo) that has complete control of "We the people" within our once sovereign states. Republicans, just like Democrats, have a vested interest in preserving the status quo from which they gain their perks, privileges, and power. The past one hundred years of American political history was a century of conservative failure—not because "We the people" were not up to the task of fighting to preserve our rights and liberties, but because the political parties claiming to represent America's conservative voters were not willing to call out the *illegitimate* supreme Federal government and work to restore America's original Republic of Sovereign States. Republicans were, and still are, more interested in gaining and maintaining their turn at controlling the power of government than they were in rolling back unconstitutional federal encroachments upon the rights reserved to "We the people." For more than a hundred years conservatives in general and Republicans (Democrats back in the day when they claimed to represent conservative voters) have never initiated a political movement that resulted in or even promised a *fundamental* reduction in the size and scope of the supreme Federal government. The productive element (law abiding, tax paying Americans) is rewarded with Republican "conservative" rhetoric, while the parasitic element is rewarded with our "redistributed" wealth! Again, always keep in mind the fact that Republican-elected officials and party bosses do not want to significantly reduce the size and scope of government—they only want their turn at the head of the supreme Federal government. Both liberal Democrat and conservative Republican politicians and party bosses have a vested interest in preserving the political status quo.

> *Keeping the "deplorables, irredeemables, and bitter clingers" pacified and dispirited is a major tactic used by America's neo-Marxist shadow government to prevent a conservative popular rebellion.*

It must be stressed that America's political establishment is designed to maintain itself by assuring incumbency for the ruling elite. The ruling elite includes the Deep State's neo-Marxist bureaucrats who control a major portion of the Federal government. These Deep State bureaucrats are unelected and therefore they answer to no one! The elite will never allow any real reform to occur because to do so would threaten their position of power, perks, and almost unlimited privileges. The Republican wing of America's political establishment can be counted on to provide occasional rhetoric scripted to fill "conservatives" with enthusiastic cheer—full of sound and fury while signifying nothing of *strategic* value.

When the cheering is over and the "good" conservatives have been sworn into office, the sad reality remains that "We the people" have elected another group of politicians, and the supreme Federal government controlled by an evil, neo-Marxist, shadow government still rules over Americans in "Podunk U.S.A." And to the discouragement of the once enthusiastic conservative voters, "We the people" must still fulfill our assigned role as humble supplicants meekly imploring our masters in Washington, DC, "Please may we have just a little more of the freedom that should be ours by birthright?"

Unfortunately, too many conservatives are slow learners, that is why we must continually make the following point to "conservatives": If we keep doing the same thing we have always done, then we should not be surprised to discover that we keep getting the same sad results. We continue to get more taxes, bigger government, and less freedom in a politically correct America. Electing "good" conservative politicians will not suffice. As long as the current political system is in place, good conservatives will most likely be turned into part of the political establishment or at best isolated, denigrated, and politically ignored until they are at last hounded out of office and replaced by loyal party members. Loyal party "boys" and "girls" are greatly appreciated in Washington, DC, because they will play by the rules established by and for the benefit of the ruling elite. The Deep State's treatment of President Trump is an example of the power exercised by America's neo-Marxist, shadow government. Statesmen and other "outsiders" cannot survive in the Deep State Swamp—the political status quo. What America needs is a strategic change in the way in which "We the people" control "our" government. This will happen only when "We the people" of the Sovereign States reclaim the Constitutional rights of nullification and secession. The only way this will occur is via the Red State-Red County Revolution!

> *If we keep doing the same thing we have always done, then we should not be surprised to find out that we will keep getting the same sad results, more taxes, bigger government, and less freedom.*

Chapter 9

Irregular Political Warfare

AS FULLY EXPLAINED in *Dixie Rising-Rules for Rebels* irregular political warfare is used by a smaller group fighting to throw-off the oppressive rule of a stronger political force. It is the opposite of "business-as-usual" politics. It is a strategic plan by which "We the people" can do an end-run around or out-flank the ruling elites in Washington, DC. As a smaller group, initially, we may not be able to elect our own people but we can make sure that those who betray us will face recall elections or are defeated in the next election. If, for example, a counterfeit conservative betrays us in the state legislature, we may well work with his Democratic opponent in the next election, causing the counterfeit conservative to lose his elected office. While this may seem terrible to those conducting business-as-usual politics, it is an excellent example of irregular political warfare. It is better to have a known opponent—who owes his election to you—at your front than to have a pretended friend "watching" your back. Irregular political warfare warriors position themselves in a manner that will allow them to punish those who dare to betray their interests and values. "We the people" must create a movement that will allow us to threaten or actually carry out such an attack against counterfeit conservatives who betray our interests. All we have to do is to do this to one or two counterfeit conservatives and *the entire herd will get the message.* Soon our so-called friends holding elected offices will begin to fear us! For the first time "our" elected officials will be facing an organized political group that is looking at the long run (strategic) impact of our actions, while they have been looking at the short run impact of the next election.

Two keys to a successful, irregular, political-warfare effort are having at least one statewide elected official in a Bully Pulpit and using him to help establish Provisional State governments in every Southern and non-Southern, American-values state.

PROVISIONAL STATE GOVERNMENTS

Provisional government, as used herein, is an organized group of individuals holding traditional, conservative, political, and moral values who work together to bring political pressure on elected officials to encourage them to protect and promote traditional, American values. The Provisional government in each state operates as a lobbying effort to kill bad legislation and to pass legislation that will further our Cause. Our lobbying effort must start at the local level and not depend upon hired lobbyists in the state legislature. The Provisional government will be similar to the Tea Party but this time we will have a strategic plan for ultimate victory! It also uses various forms of public information to educate the public about the necessity of standing firm against America's neo-Marxist enemies. It is also responsible for educating the public about the virtue of and necessity for reclaiming our Constitutional rights of nullification and secession. Our Provisional governments serve as the counter-balance to the evil, politically correct, neo-Marxist, shadow government that currently controls America, while working for a *fundamental* change in the way in which "We the people" control our Federal government.

Provisional Governments in each state have three primary purposes:

> 1. Educate and arouse the public through a statewide public relations campaign via social media, radio ads, and local rallies, etc.,

2. Organizing at the local level and then lobby the state legislature to defeat legislation that poses a threat to American values and enact legislation that supports traditional, conservative, American values. This "lobbying" effort is radically different from the classic lobbying efforts based upon hiring a professional lobbyist. Our lobbying strength is based upon local groups working to bring political and social pressure on their elected officials in the legislature, and

3. Promote South-wide and non-Southern Red State ballot initiatives demanding passage of our Sovereign State Amendment to U.S. Constitution.[1]

Provisional governments in each state take the place of spending enormous amounts of money running "our" candidates for elected office. Instead of trying to elect a majority of the members of the state legislature, we use our Provisional government to influence the killing or passing of legislation necessary for our movement. We do not spend enormous amounts of scarce resources in an endless and usually fruitless effort to gain political office. Instead, we organize a Provisional government to influence (pressure) elected officials in the state legislature to vote against legislation harmful to our American and Southern values and eventually enact legislation necessary to place our Sovereign State Amendment before the people of our state. In the meantime, we continue to "educate to motivate" the general public, slowly turning them from passive conservatives into first supporters and eventually active voters and workers for the Cause of regaining a Constitutionally-limited Republic of Sovereign States. This is the essential work of irregular political warriors. We use the political system, but we do not engage our political enemies in a traditional political campaign. We do not engage in the traditional election cycle. Instead, we find a few opportunities to unite behind our select candidate—we

---

1 Copy of our Sovereign State Amendment to the U.S. Constitution in Chapter 12.

carefully select one state-wide office for which we will run one of our own. This is a limited but **strategic** move to secure a "Bully Pulpit" for our movement.

THE BULLY PULPIT—WHAT IS IT?

As explained in *Dixie Rising-Rules for Rebels*, the Bully Pulpit is a state-wide elected office in which the incumbent uses the prestige of the office to advance the Cause of American Constitutional liberty by the ratification of our Sovereign State Amendment or, if necessary, Red State-Red County secession. Secession is the last option but, if necessary, "We the people" will establish a country of our own. The elected official in the Bully Pulpit becomes the spokesman for the Cause not only in his state but across the South and the nation. He will be key in the effort to organize pro-liberty folks in every Southern state and other Red States and Red Counties in non-Southern states. By virtue of his office, he establishes our movement as a legitimate political effort, he will generate public interest, knowledge and enthusiasm for our Cause.

THE BULLY PULPIT—WHY DO WE NEED IT?

The destruction of our Christian, conservative, Southern heritage and the ongoing efforts to disarm law-abiding Americans is not due to a lack of pro-Southern, pro-American values, books, blogs, or scholarly lectures. The source of our problem is that our neo-Marxist enemies have captured the political establishment and are using it to destroy traditional, Southern and American values. Only political power can counter political power. They have power, we do not! One person in a Bully Pulpit would capture the imagination of the conservative public and encourage them to join our movement to defeat America's neo-Marxist enemies. Southerners and other Americans will follow a strong, visionary, leader who uses his Bully Pulpit to organize a mass movement; a leader who has developed a *strategic* plan to defeat the neo-Marxist mobs and replace the current illegitimate, supreme Federal government with a Constitutional Republic of Sovereign

States. In the new America our rights and the limitations on Federal power inscribed in the Constitution will be enforced by real States' Rights including the rights of state nullification and secession. "We the people" must develop a political mechanism to enforce the protections enumerated in the Constitution. Always remember that the Constitution is not self-enforcing. By using irregular political warfare, establishing Provisional governments, and capturing a Bully Pulpit, we can create the power to enforce the limitations imposed on the Federal government by the Constitution or, if necessary, create a nation of our own—a nation that recognizes traditional, American values such as the right to keep and bear arms.

WHO DO WE TRUST TO FILL THE BULLY PULPIT?

The individual in the Bully Pulpit must be "one of us." Someone who is not a career politician, someone who will spend his time advancing our Cause—not someone who is advancing his political career. The individual must understand the necessity of using irregular political warfare to unseat the political status quo. Someone who understands that the status quo political system is designed to favor the ruling elites, while holding "We the people" as political slaves. American-values voters must begin to work together to raise the money necessary to contest and win a statewide office, select the targeted office, select the correct individual to fill the office and flood the state with the finances and volunteers needed to elect "our" candidate. Once the initial Bully Pulpit is secured, irregular political warfare can begin in earnest.

CONDUCTING IRREGULAR POLITICAL WARFARE IN STATE LEGISLATURES

While the national aim of our Provisional governments is to pursue the submission to the states and eventual ratification of our Sovereign State Amendment, we will also be pursuing numerous legislative initiatives in state legislatures. We will encourage "conservative" legislators to introduce legislation that would be beneficial to the cause of preserving and promoting traditional, American values. For example, we will support freedom of speech in public education institutions. We will introduce riders to bills providing tax revenues for public universities requiring them to allow academic credits for attending university-sponsored lectures promoting traditional, American values such as the right to keep and bear arms. Such law would also, provide for harsh punishment for students, facility, or outsiders who attempt to disrupt these lectures. We will introduce legislation defining "racism" as the advocacy of using racial distinctions to deny equal rights under the law. Anyone accusing an individual (typically neo-Marxists slandering conservatives) of being a racist, etc. without providing supporting evidence that the individual they labeled as a racist meets the statutory definition of racist, the accuser will be guilty of slander and such slander will be treated as a hate crime. We will also seek new laws requiring strict enforcement of voter identification and policing of voter registration rolls. Individuals, elected or appointed, who are responsible for maintaining the integrity of the voting rolls will be personally liable to class action suits by aggrieved voters to determine if they intentionally or negligently failed to perform their duties to maintain the integrity of the state's voting system.

State legislators, as with all politicians, respond to pressure, especially when it comes from their local constituents. This is why the Provisional government must spend a great deal of time and effort at the local level via radio, newspaper, and social media advertisements promoting our cause. An American-values lobbyist in the state legislature is useless without back-up in the local counties. People at the local level must understand what we are doing in the state's legislature and why we are doing it. They must feel that they are a part of the movement to restore true, conservative, American values. As explained in *Dixie Rising-Rules for Rebels* we must first educate our fellow Americans, then turn them into supporters and eventually into activists fighting to reclaim our country or, if necessary, to create a nation of our own.

Chapter 10

WHY WE NEED THE SOVEREIGN STATE AMENDMENT

RATIFYING OUR PROPOSED Sovereign State Amendment would result in a *fundamental* change in American government. It would be a revolutionary change but it would be a conservative revolutionary change! It would be a change back to the Constitutional principles advocated by the Founding Fathers. It would be a Constitutionally-limited Federal government that would be forced, by the Sovereign States, to function within its constitutionally limited authority. Decisions of the Federal Courts would be persuasive and followed in all but the most extreme cases. The Supreme Court's decision would not be mandatory. The Sovereign State could nullify any Federal Court decision if it violates or infringes upon the rights of the state's citizens. The existence of the clearly acknowledged rights of nullification and secession will tend to reduce federal abuse of our rights. It serves as a check against federal overreach.

The potential for federal/state conflict is reduced because Congress would be reluctant to pass laws that would be opposed by large numbers of Americans (a distinct contrast between the way Congress rammed health care reform, aka Obamacare, "down our throats"). In addition, the Federal Supreme Court would be reluctant to issue decisions that they know "We the people" within our sovereign state(s) would immediately nullify. For example, the

> ## THE CURRENT SUPREME FEDERAL GOVERNMENT ENCOURAGES A HAUGHTY STYLE OF GOVERNMENT BORDERING ON TYRANNY.

Supreme Court's overturning of the Defense of Marriage Act would have never occurred if "We the people" had the power to nullify such Supreme Court orders. The same principle holds true for outrageous Executive Orders issued by a power-hungry president. The rights of nullification and secession encourage mutual respect and toleration between diverse sections of the United States. This is the form of Federal government our Founding Father created when they proposed and the sovereign states ratified the original Constitution. This is radically different from the current unconstitutional, and therefore *illegitimate*, system we currently live under. The current system encourages a haughty style of government that borders on tyranny—and during the Chinese Communist COVID-19 virus crises federal and state governments actually crossed the border of tyranny.

THIS IS A STRATEGIC PLAN FOR VICTORY—THE DESTRUCTION OF NEO-MARXIST RULING ELITES

With the 1991 publication of the first edition of *The South Was Right!*[1] the Kennedy Twins of Louisiana boldly proclaimed that there must be a political solution to the ongoing campaign of

---

1 The first edition of *The South Was Right* was published in 1991, the second edition in 1994, and the third edition in 2020. Each subsequent edition was updated and enlarged. It has sold over 140,000 copies.

anti-South, cultural genocide. We warned that the attack against Southern heritage and heroes is a precursor to a much greater attack against all American values.

In 1994 we released the second edition of *The South Was Right* in which we suggested that the South take the lead in seeking a political solution to an out-of-control Federal government. This was the first time a strategic plan for ultimate victory has been suggested. For over a quarter of a century the "leadership" of the South has failed to protect our religious, cultural and political liberty. Our "leaders" have left us defenseless while evil, neo-Marxists viciously assaulted traditional, Southern and American values. We now have an opportunity to launch a counter-attack against our enemies. We now have an opportunity to reclaim America's original Constitutionally-limited Republic of Sovereign States.

More detailed information about the Bully Pulpit, irregular political warfare, Provisional Government, South-wide ballot initiatives, and our Sovereign State Amendment to the U.S. Constitution can be found in the second edition (2021) *Dixie Rising-Rules for Rebels*. And for non-Southerners who don't think the term "Rebels" would apply to them, remember that the Tories and British called our colonial ancestor "Rebels." Those American Rebels rose in 1776 and won our freedom and today's Rebels will rise again and win our freedom. Our aim is not just to win an election. Our aim is to make a *fundamental* change in the way the Federal government is controlled and thereby win Freedom for all traditional Americans who want to live in a free nation!

YOU ARE KEY TO INITIATING THIS REVOLUTION

The Red State-Red County revolution needs a spokesman in an elected office to assist development of Provisional governments in all Red States and Red Counties. The first Bully Pulpit will be the start of Provisional Governments in every Red State and Red County currently being held captive in Blue States. It will be the beginning of efforts to encourage conservative counties in Blue States to establish pro-American-values sanctuary counties in liberal (Blue) states! "We the people" have allowed ourselves to become the neo-Marxist shadow government's political slaves. They are convinced that we have no other choice but to obey their dictates. It is up to us to join together, form our Provisional governments, and initiate irregular political warfare—the Red State-Red County, American-values revolution.

IT IS NOT AN ELECTION—IT IS A REVOLUTION TO DESTROY THE DEEP STATE

Elections in modern America are merely a means by which "We the people" are allowed to select politically connected individuals who will manage America's decline. The Red State-Red County movement is about initiating a revolution to reclaim America's original, Constitutionally-limited, Republic of Sovereign States. It is about expelling the self-appointed ruling elite in Washington, DC's Deep State and returning the right of self-government to the people within their states and local communities.

Electing one of our own to a statewide office, the office of Lt. Governor for example, will be the beginning of a South-wide and non-Southern Red States/Red Counties movement. It is a movement that champions conservative, American values that will offer hope not only to Southerners but to Americans in conservative counties and states across America. "We the people" must initiate the revolt against the unelected bureaucrats in the Deep State, the financial elites on Wall Street, the neo-Marxist media elites, and America's political ruling-class. This revolt begins with the establishing of Provisional governments and the electing of one of our own to a statewide office—someone we can count on to use his office as the initial Bully Pulpit for our movement. As our movement grows, we will establish Provisional governments in all other Red States and Red Counties within Blue States. Soon we will have many of our own folks elected to Bully Pulpits in various states. This is important because if a movement is based on one charismatic individual, then one bullet can end the movement. Recall how Huey Long's nationwide movement in the 1930s came to an end with his assassination. The same thing happened to

George Wallace's nationwide movement when he was shot. (I am not necessarily endorsing the ideas advocated by either one of these movements but they both serve as examples of why our movement will eventually need more than one person in a Bully Pulpit.)

We will encourage the establishment of conservative, American-values, sanctuary counties in liberal states; encourage those counties to secede from liberal states and form their own, self-governing conservative states; we will place before voters in Southern and non-Southern states a ballot initiative demanding that the Federal Congress submit to the states a Constitutional Amendment (the Sovereign State Amendment) acknowledging the right of state nullification and secession.

Chapter 11

RED COUNTY AMERICAN-VALUES SANCTUARY COUNTIES

RED STATE PROVISIONAL governments will support and encourage American-values voters residing in Red Counties within Blue States to establish American-values sanctuary counties. For example, if the neo-Marxist-controlled state legislature in Virginia or Oregon attempts to violate the right to keep and bear arms, then Red Counties in Virginia or Oregon should hold a county ballot initiative declaring their county to be a Second Amendment sanctuary county. Seven counties in Oregon have already voted to secede from Oregon and join Idaho as of May, 2021.[1] The primary function of such actions is to keep the issue of local self-government before the American people. Such irregular political warfare efforts will force the supreme Federal government and its puppet state government to "show its hand" as an oppressive tyranny when it sends federal marshals into American counties to force compliance with illegitimate Blue State laws. Provisional governments will make sure every nation in the world is informed about the imperialistic acts of America's neo-Marxist Federal and state governments. Political action at the local level will be used to foster a mass political movement. As demonstrated in *Dixie*

---

1   https://www.oregonlive.com/politics/2021/05/more-oregon-counties-vote-to-move-into-idaho-part-of-rural-effort-to-to-gain-political-refuge-from-blue-states.html accessed 8/8/2021.

Rising-Rules for Rebels many people living in a captive nation have used non-violent, massive, civil-disobedience tactics to gain their freedom—there is no reason that American-values voters in Red States and Red Counties cannot do the same!

RED COUNTY SECESSION FROM BLUE STATES

A look at a 2020 presidential election map showing Red (conservative votes) and Blue (liberal votes) counties will quickly demonstrate that there are large numbers of Red Counties in Blue States where the voters support conservative candidates and issues. Unfortunately, in Blue States the American-values voters in Red Counties are dominated by—as in ruled by—neo-Marxists who control their state's legislative, executive, and judicial branches of government. For example, California's Red Counties are dominated by neo-Marxists in vast urban areas along the Pacific coast. By holding ballot initiatives to declare these counties as American-values sanctuary counties, the neo-Marxists holding state power will be put on notice that if they reject the attempt to establish American-values sanctuary counties, then these counties will begin a Red County secession movement with the goal of establishing East California as a new state. If Congress refuses to accept East California as a member of the Union, then East California and other "orphan states" will join the Red State secession movement as we work to create a nation of our own.

SECESSION AS A BARGAINING TOOL

A reading of our Sovereign State Constitutional Amendment will demonstrate that our first aim is not secession but a restoration of America's original, Constitutionally-limited Republic of Sovereign States. As noted in *Dixie Rising-Rules for Rebels* unsuccessful secession movements in other captive nations still had a positive impact that produced favorable social and political outcomes for the captive nations. Quebec had several failed efforts to secede from Canada. The Canadian Federal government made numerous concessions to the French-speaking citizens of Quebec to convince them to remain in the Canadian Union. Secession is a good goal but it can also be a great bargaining tool—never throw away a useful tool. The *viable* threat of secession is a useful tool that American-values voters in Red States and Red Counties must learn to use.

SECESSION AS THE FINAL RESORT

American-values voters (conservative, Red State, Red County voters) must take the same stand that Patrick Henry took when it comes to preserving the Union. He made it clear that liberty always trumps government when he declared, "The first thing I have at heart is American *liberty*, the second is American *union*." American Constitutional liberty is our goal—not secession. But secession is the final resort if our neo-Marxist enemies refuse to allow "We the people" the right of local self-government. We must hang our neo-Marxist enemies on the horns of a dilemma—either they ratify our Sovereign State Amendment or else face a nation-wide secession movement. And they will be well served to remember President John F. Kennedy's admonition, "Those who make peaceful revolution impossible will make violent revolution inevitable."

Chapter 12

OUR SOVEREIGN STATE
CONSTITUTIONAL AMENDMENT

THE FOLLOWING is our Sovereign State Constitutional Amendment. It must be stressed that this amendment does not create new rights for Americans—it only makes it absolutely clear that the Federal government acknowledges these unalienable rights belonging to "We the people" within our Sovereign States.

THE SOVEREIGN STATE AMENDMENT

These United States of America are a Republic of Sovereign States. The federal government derives its authority from the consent of the governed residing within their respective Sovereign State. Each Sovereign State is the agent of the people thereof. The federal government formed by the compact of the United States Constitution is the agent of the Sovereign States. Federal authority shall be supreme in all areas specifically delegated to it by the Constitution. All acts or legislation enacted pursuant to the Constitution shall be the supreme law of the land. Each Sovereign State, as with all Sovereigns, reserves the right to judge for itself as to the constitutionality of any act of its agent, the federal government.

Section I. Each Sovereign State specifically reserves the right to interpose its sovereign authority between acts of the federal government and the liberties, property, and interests of the citizens of the state, thereby nullifying federal acts judged by the state to be an unwarranted infringement upon the reserved rights of the state and the people thereof.

1. State nullification of a federal act must be approved by a convention of the state.

2. Upon passage of an act of nullification, all federal authority for the enumerated and nullified act(s) shall be suspended within the nullifying state.

3. Upon formal acceptance of nullification by three-fourths of the conventions of the states, including the original nullifying state, the enumerated federal act(s) shall be prohibited in the United States of America and its territories.

4. Upon formal rejection of nullification by three-fourths of the conventions of the states, the enumerated federal act(s) shall be presumed to be constitutional, notwithstanding any judgment of any federal or state court.

5. Until or unless there is a formal approval or rejection by the conventions of the states, the nullified federal act(s) shall remain non-operative as to the original and any additional nullifying states. A state that in its convention ratifies a particular act of nullification, naming the same or similar acts nullified by the original state's act of nullification, shall be construed to have nullified the same act as enumerated in the initiating state's nullification.

6. No federal elected official, agent, or any individual working within or associated with any branch of the federal government may

harass or attempt to harass, intimidate, or threaten a Sovereign State or the people thereof for exercising their rights under this amendment. No federal elected official, agent, or any individual working within or associated with any branch of the federal government shall attempt to influence or use their office to attempt to influence the deliberations of the people regarding the nullification of a federal act(s) or the acceptance or rejection of a nullified federal act(s).

7. Any United States military officer, non-commissioned officer or federal official or agent who carries out or attempts to carry out any order by a federal official, officer or agent to deny or hinder the people of a Sovereign State from exercising their rights under this amendment shall be subject to the offended state's laws and may be tried accordingly. Jurisdiction in such cases is specifically denied to all federal courts, military courts, or any other court other than the courts of the offended state.

Section II. The government and people of these United States approve the principle that any people have a right to abolish the existing government and form a new one that suits them better. This principle illustrates the American idea that government rests on the consent of the governed and that it is the right of a people to alter or abolish it at will whenever it becomes destructive of the ends for which it was established. Therefore, the right of a Sovereign State to secede peacefully from the union voluntarily created by the compact of the Constitution is hereby specifically reserved to each state.

1. An act of secession shall be executed by a convention of the people of the state.

2. The seceded state shall appoint representatives to negotiate settlement of all debts owed the federal government, the purchase of federal properties within the Sovereign state, and the removal of federal military installations and personnel.

3. Upon acceptable arrangement for the payment of sums owed the federal government, the representatives may negotiate treaties of friendship, common defense, and commercial relations. Said treaties are subject to the same constitutional ratification as other treaties.

4. Readmission of a seceded state shall follow the same constitutional requirements as for any new state.

5. No federal elected official, agent, or any individual working within or associated with any branch of the federal government shall attempt to influence the people of the Sovereign State regarding their decision to secede from, remain with, or join this union.

6. Any United States military officer, non-commissioned officer, or federal official or agent who carries out or attempts to carry out any order by a federal official, officer, or agent to deny or hinder the people of a Sovereign State from exercising their rights under this amendment shall be subject to the offended state's laws and may be tried accordingly. Jurisdiction in such cases is specifically denied to all federal courts, military courts, or any other court other than the courts of the offended state.

The duty of the people of the Sovereign State to exercise their inalienable right to govern themselves is a right that existed before the formation of the federal government, and therefore nothing in this amendment shall be interpreted in such a manner as to deem the federal government to be the donor of the rights as exercised by the people of the states.

This home-made sign, "Looters will be shot," was posted by citizens during the aftermath of Hurricane Ida (2021). During a natural disaster law enforcement may become overwhelmed, homes are left vacant, and private security systems are off-line. During such times it is the responsibility of armed citizens to protect themselves, their families, and their property. America's Founding Fathers did not create the 2nd Amendment just so that Jim Bob and Bubba could go squirrel hunting. The 2nd Amendment was created to allow citizens to protect themselves from criminals and tyrants!

Chapter 13

SUMMARY—
TIME TO TURN OUR WORDS INTO ACTION

OUR SECOND AMENDMENT rights are under attack. The same neo-Marxist enemy that is attempting to disarm law-abiding Americans is also busy destroying all traditional, conservative, moral, and political values. America's neo-Marxists are a part of an international neo-Marxist movement aimed at destroying Western Christian civilization and replacing it with their version of a Marxist utopia. Truth to a neo-Marxist is anything that promotes their longed-for Marxist revolution, while falsehood is anything that tends to hinder their movement. We cannot win by debating these people because their standard of truth is radically different from our standard of truth.[1] We cannot fight them using standard political tactics such as relying on electing "good" conservatives—after over a century of conservative failure we should at last understand this fact.

One hundred years of conservative failure proves the reality of the truism, "The Constitution is not self-enforcing." We cannot protect our rights by relying on the words in the Constitution because without a political means to enforce those words, the Constitution becomes a mere paper barricade. If we are to win in this great struggle for freedom, we must engage our neo-Marxist

---

1 See **Yankee Empire-Where Truth No Longer Matters** Addendum XI, Kennedy & Kennedy, *The South Was Right! 3rd edition*, 471-6.

enemy in irregular political warfare. As pointed out in *Dixie Rising-Rules for Rebels* many countries in recent history have won their independence or at least forced an oppressive central government to withdraw its oppressive acts and leave the local people alone. It remains to be seen if "We the people" are willing to take the audacious stand for freedom that our colonial ancestors were willing to take for us back in 1776.

Deo Vindice

About the Author

JAMES RONALD KENNEDY was born in Mississippi and moved to Louisiana in1973. Ron and this twin brother Donnie have authored 17 books including the bestselling book *The South Was Right!* which sold more than 140,000; the third edition was released in 2020. The following Kennedy Twin's books are in current publication: *Yankee Empire: Aggressive Abroad and Despotic at Home; Rawle's View of the Constitution-Secession as Taught at West Point; Punished With Poverty-the Suffering South.* Ron's books include, *Dixie Rising-Rules for Rebels; When Rebel Was Cool-Growing-Up in Dixie; Red State-Red County Revolution; Be Ye Separate—Bible Belt Revival or Revolution;* and, *Nullifying Gun Control.*

Ron is past Division Commander, Louisiana Sons of Confederate Veterans (SCV), in 2018 he was appointed Deputy of Heritage Promotions National SCV. He is a frequent speaker at SCV, Southern Heritage and other pro-Liberty groups. Ron received a Master in Health Administration (MHA) from Tulane University in New Orleans, a Master of Jurisprudence in Healthcare Law (MJ) from Loyola University, Chicago, and a Bachelor's degree from University of Louisiana Monroe. He retired in April 2015 after serving over 20 years as Vice-President of Risk Management for a Louisiana-based insurance company.

AUTHORS' WEBSITE: WWW.KENNEDYTWINS.COM

Books By The Kennedy Twins

IN CURRENT PUBLICATION

Jefferson Davis: High Road to Emancipation and Constitutional Government (2022)

Nullifying Federal and State Gun Control (2021)

Dixie Rising-Rules for Rebels, (2nd edition 2021, 1st edition 2017)

The South Was Right!, 3rd edition, (2020, 1st edition 1991, 2nd edition 1994)

Punished With Poverty-The Suffering South, (2nd edition 2020, 1st edition 2016)

Yankee Empire: Aggressive Abroad and Despotic at Home, (2018)

A View of the Constitution-Secession Taught At West Point (2nd edition 2020 1st 1993)

Confederate Myth Buster, (2019)

Red State-Red County Secession (2020)

Be Ye Separate: Bible Belt Revival or Marxist Revolution (2021)

When Rebel Was Cool-Growing Up In Dixie (2020)

OUT OF PRINT

Why Not Freedom! (1995)

Myths of American Slavery (2003)

Reclaiming Liberty (2005)

Was Jefferson Davis Right? (2010, Updated and republished 2022 as *Jefferson Davis: High Road to Emancipation and Constitutional Government*)

Nullification: Why and How (2010)

Lincoln's Marxists (2011)

Nullifying Tyranny (2012)

Uncle Seth Fought the Yankees (2015)

Rekilling Lincoln (2015)